AF228357

Enduro Racing

Rev it Up!

Brianna Kaiser

Lerner Publications • Minneapolis

Lerner Publications Company
An imprint of Lerner Publishing Group, Inc.
241 First Avenue North
Minneapolis, MN 55401 USA

For reading levels and more information, look up this title at www.lernerbooks.com.

Main body text set in Billy Infant Regular. Typeface provided by SparkType.

Editor: Lauren Foley

Library of Congress Cataloging-in-Publication Data

Names: Kaiser, Brianna, 1996- author.
Title: Enduro racing : rev it up! / Brianna Kaiser.
Description: Minneapolis : Lerner Publications, 2023. | Series: Lightning bolt books. Dirt bike zone | Includes bibliographical references and index. | Audience: Ages 6–9 | Audience: Grades 2–3 | Summary: "Enduro racing is all about endurance. From the gear and terrain to famous racers, zip into the world of Enduro in this exciting introduction to the sport"— Provided by publisher.
Identifiers: LCCN 2022011642 (print) | LCCN 2022011643 (ebook) | ISBN 9781728476292 (library binding) | ISBN 9781728478715 (paperback) | ISBN 9781728483146 (ebook)
Subjects: LCSH: Motocross—Juvenile literature.
Classification: LCC GV1060.12 .K34 2023 (print) | LCC GV1060.12 (ebook) | DDC 796.7/56—dc23/eng/20220421

LC record available at https://lccn.loc.gov/2022011642
LC ebook record available at https://lccn.loc.gov/2022011643

Manufactured in the United States of America
1-52210-50650-5/11/2022

Table of Contents

Cruising Downhill

You zip downhill in timed stages. The race through the woods will last hours, but you came prepared. You're in an Enduro race!

Enduro is a type of dirt bike race. Dirt bikes are motorcycles that are made only for off-road riding.

All about Enduro

Enduro racing is similar to mountain biking. One kind of Enduro racing even uses mountain bikes. But many Enduro riders race dirt bikes.

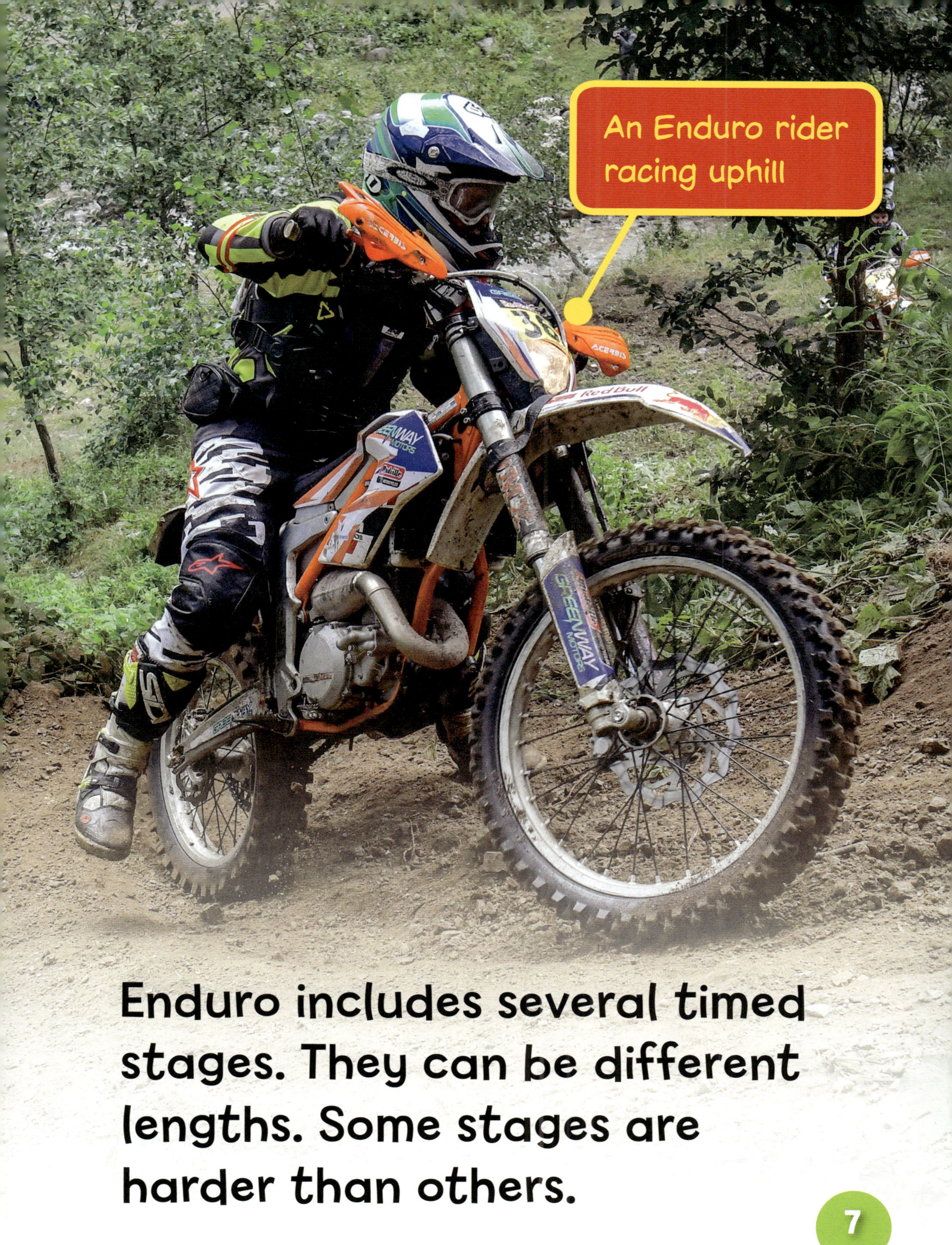

Enduro includes several timed stages. They can be different lengths. Some stages are harder than others.

Riders race in small groups of about three to five people. They have to arrive to the race and checkpoints on time. They can lose points for showing up too late or too early.

Once the race begins, riders follow a marked course. The courses include rough terrain. Riders can race through the woods or deserts.

Enduro racing can include rough terrain like rocks.

A rider's scores are recorded at different checkpoints throughout the race. At the end of the race, all their scores are combined. The rider with the best score wins.

Three riders celebrating their wins after the Motul Roof of Africa, a yearly Enduro race

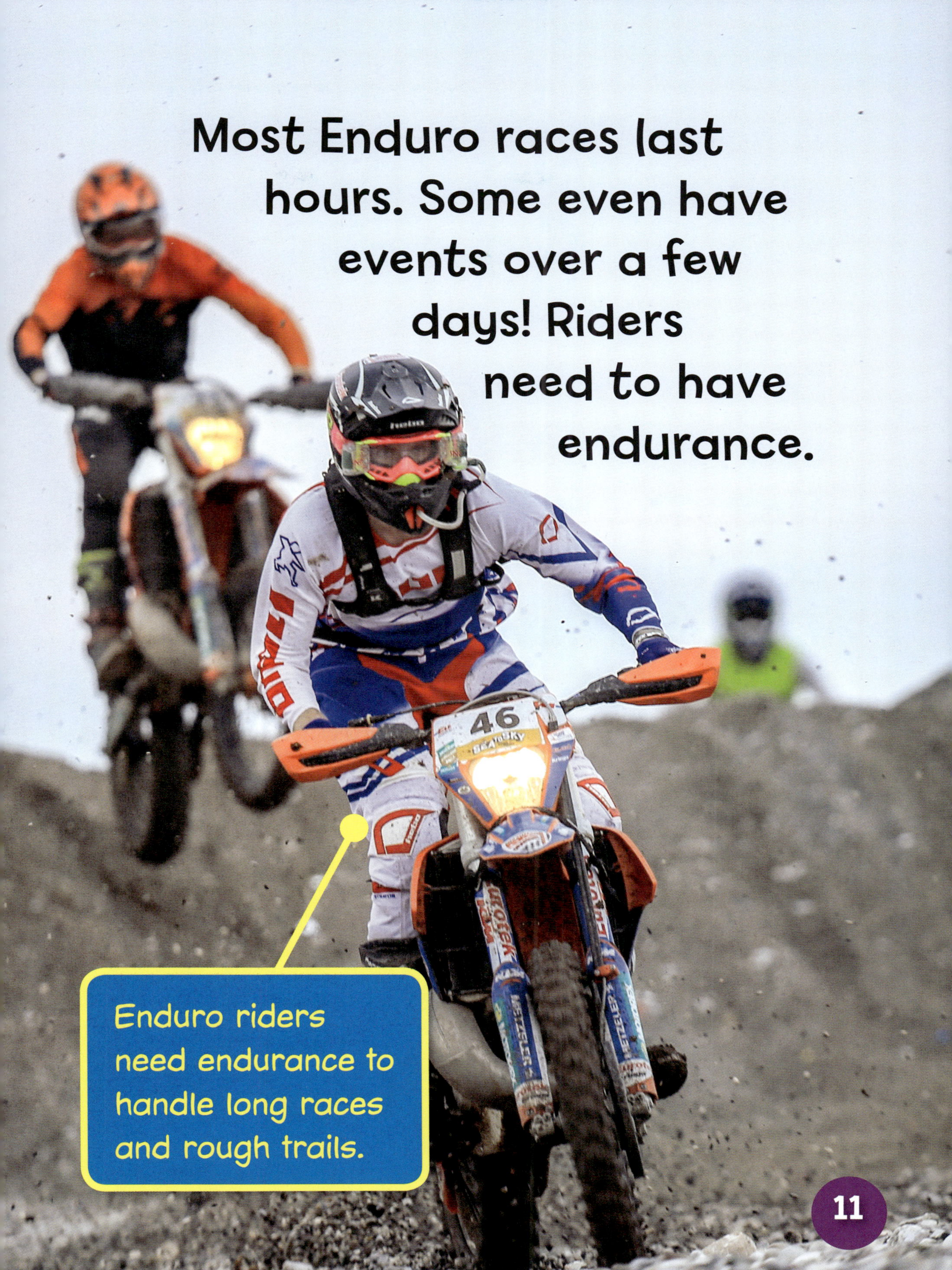

Most Enduro races last
hours. Some even have
events over a few
days! Riders
need to have
endurance.

Enduro riders
need endurance to
handle long races
and rough trails.

11

Racing Gear

Enduro riders have many brands of bikes to choose from. The bikes have tires that can handle rough terrain. They also have strong brakes.

The bikes have handguards too. These protect the rider's hands from branches during a race.

Riders wear gear and body armor to protect themselves. They wear special jackets and pants, gloves, and boots. They also wear neck and knee braces, a helmet, and goggles.

A dirt bike helmet with goggles in place

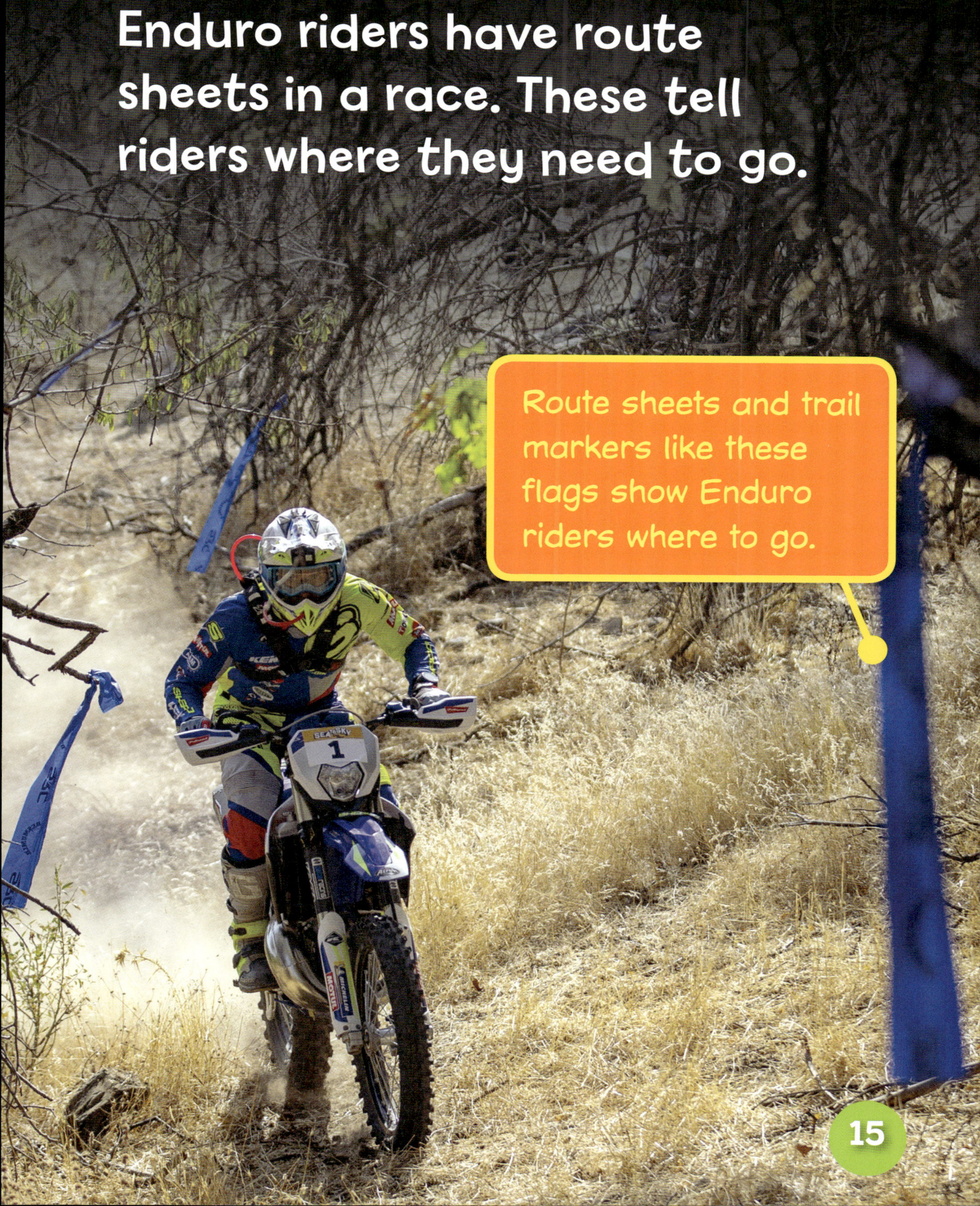

Enduro riders have route sheets in a race. These tell riders where they need to go.

15

Enduro Stars and Events

Riders compete in Enduro races all over the world. The Gotland Grand National in Sweden is the biggest Enduro competition in the world. The race is about 14 miles (22 km) long and lasts three hours.

Kirsten Landman of South Africa is one of Africa's top female Enduro racers. She was the first woman to finish certain races, including Redbull Sea to Sky.

Jane Daniels of Britain has been riding in Enduro races since she was twelve. She won the Women's World Cup Championship in 2019 and 2020.

Josep García of Spain comes from a family of bikers. He has won many races, including first-place wins each year from 2018 through 2021. Fans will see what these riders and others will accomplish in the future.

Josep García riding in an Enduro race

Bike Diagram
KTM 250 EXC

How it Works

Enduro races are partly downhill, so brakes are very important. Dirt bikes have front and rear brakes. Mainly, the front brake is for stopping and the rear brake is for control. Enduro riders want to make good times to win the race. One way to make good time is by being fast on turns. Riders that brake with control can make better and faster turns than their opponents.

Glossary

accomplish: to complete or carry out

armor: a strong material worn to protect the body

combine: to add or join into a whole

compete: to try to win an event

endurance: the strength and ability needed to last in something such as an Enduro race

off-road: riding on rough roads, such as dirt or sand

stage: a period of an Enduro race

terrain: an area of land and its natural characteristics and surface

Learn More

American Motorcyclist Association: Enduro
https://americanmotorcyclist.com/enduro/

Extreme: MotoX Motocross
https://www.ducksters.com/sports/extrememotox
.php

Hogan, Christa C. *Mountain Biking*. Minneapolis: SportsZone, 2020.

Kaiser, Brianna. *Cross Country Dirt Bike Racing: Rev It Up!* Minneapolis: Lerner Publications, 2023.

Mikoley, Kate. *Off-Road Racing*. New York: Gareth Stevens, 2020.

Motorcycle Racing Facts for Kids
https://kids.kiddle.co/Motorcycle_racing

Index

Photo Acknowledgments

Image credits: sportpoint/Shutterstock, p. 4; Oktay Ozden/Anadolu Agency/Getty Images, p. 5; Nika Lerman/Alamy Stock Photo, p. 6; Weblogiq/Shutterstock, p. 7; Pau Buera/Alamy Stock Photo, p. 8; Orhan Cicek/Anadolu Agency/Getty Images, p. 9; AP Photo/Tyrone Bradley/Red Bull Content Pool, p. 10; Mustafa Ciftci/Anadolu Agency/Getty Images, pp. 11, 15, 17; Oleg Izyum/Shutterstock, p. 12; Aleksey Suvorov/Alamy Stock Photo, p. 13; maradon 333/Shutterstock, p. 14; AP Photo/Maja Suslin/TT Nyhetsbyrån, p. 16; Adrian Dennis/AFP/Getty Images, p. 18; AP Photo/Tommi Anttonen/Lehtikuva, p. 19; otomobil/Shutterstock, p. 20.

Cover: AP Photo/Tyrone Bradley/Red Bull Content Pool.